TASTE THE WORLD!

TOMATO

WORLD BOOK

www.worldbook.com

TABLE OF CONTENTS

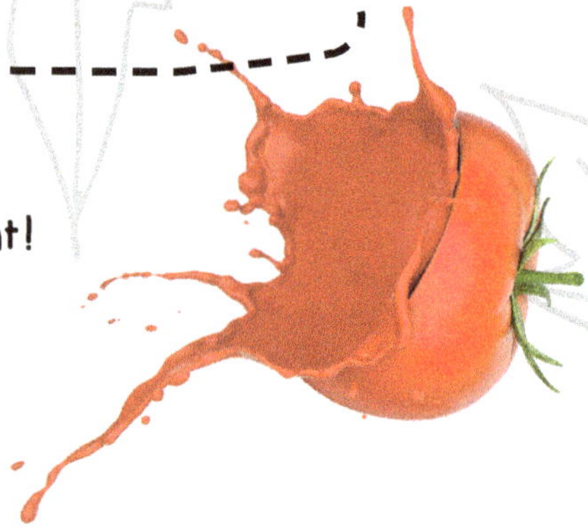

BEFORE YOU BEGIN

Included in this book are a few recipes that allow you to "taste the world!" Before you begin, look on page 46 for some helpful hints. Read the recipes carefully and always ask an adult to help–especially when handling knives or using the stove. Besides, cooking is easier and more fun when you work together!

ARE YOU HUNGRY FOR AN ADVENTURE IN FOOD? LET'S TAKE A TASTY TRIP AROUND THE WORLD TO LEARN ALL ABOUT ME...

We will explore my history, discover some fun facts, and learn to prepare some delicious recipes along the way.

As we travel around the world, you may read words that are new to you. If I can explain what a word means easily, I'll do it right where you are reading. If I use the word many times, or if the explanation is complicated, I will put the word in **boldface** (type that **looks like this**). Boldface words are defined in a glossary in the back of the book.

WHAT IS A

TOMATO?

Tomato plants are grown for their smooth, round, juicy fruit. Fresh tomatoes are eaten raw or cooked in a variety of dishes. Tomatoes are also used to make food products. These products include **ketchup,** spaghetti sauce, tomato juice, tomato soup, and tomato sauce. Tomatoes are an important source of vitamins and minerals.

FRUIT OR VEGGIE?

Some people, such as *botanists* (scientists who study plants), classify tomatoes as fruits. Botanists define fruit as the part of a flowering plant that contains the seeds.

But others, such as *horticulturists* (experts in growing plants), classify tomatoes as vegetables. This is because fresh tomatoes are used in much the same way we use cauliflower, lettuce, onions, and many other vegetables.

WHAT DO YOU THINK THEY ARE?

A FEDERAL CASE

On May 10, 1893, the U.S. Supreme Court declared that the tomato is a vegetable. This is because vegetables are usually eaten as a main course rather than as a dessert.

A CLOSER LOOK AT THE TOMATO PLANT. . .

The plant spreads out as it grows. It has a strong smell. The plants typically grow 3 to 10 feet (1 to 3 meters) in height. They produce small yellow flowers that later form tomatoes. Tomatoes are green at first and change color as they ripen. The common eating tomato turns a rich red.

The word *tomato* refers both to the fruit and to the entire plant.

Tomato seeds need 75 to 85 days to develop into mature plants with ripe fruits. Tomatoes may be grown indoors or outdoors.

Tomatoes grow well in fertile, warm, well-drained soil. They grow best in locations that receive at least six hours of direct sunlight each day. Tomatoes are popular with home gardeners because they will grow in nearly any kind of soil.

DID YOU KNOW that many people were afraid to eat tomatoes because they are related to several poisonous plants in the nightshade family? But don't be afraid: the fruit of the tomato is perfectly safe to eat! The family also includes such vegetables as eggplants and potatoes.

There are small hairs on the stem.

WOLF PEACH

The scientific name for tomato is *Lycopersicon lycopersicum,* which means *wolf peach.* It stems from old German folklore. It was believed that members of the nightshade family were used by witches to produce werewolves!

TYPES OF

TOMATOES

People grow hundreds of **varieties** (kinds) of tomatoes. They come in many different sizes, shapes, and a rainbow of colors.

BEST FRESH

To enjoy the most flavor from tomatoes, eat them freshly picked. Do not put them in the refrigerator: the cold weakens their taste.

Heirloom tomatoes are *pollinated* (fertilized) by insects. Their seeds have not changed and have been passed down through many generations. Heirloom tomatoes have a very rich flavor.

Black tomatoes have a smoky flavor. Yellow or orange tomatoes have a milder taste.

Researchers and growers have bred tomatoes to increase the number of fruits per plant and to improve their quality and other features. They sometimes breed two different varieties of tomatoes to bring out the best features of each in a new plant. These plants are called **hybrids.**

DID YOU KNOW that the size of a tomato can affect its flavor? It's true! There is a higher concentration of sugar in a smaller tomato.

TOMATOES ORIGINATED IN

SOUTH AMERICA

Tomatoes first grew as wild plants in the Andes Mountains area of northern Peru, southern Ecuador, and Bolivia over 20,000 years ago.

The first tomatoes were very small—about the size of a pea. They had a sweet-tart flavor. But there is no evidence that the people who lived there at the time ever ate them.

GRANDFATHER OF ALL TOMATOES

The wild ancestor of all the tomatoes we eat today can still be found growing wild in northern Peru and southern Ecuador.

SEEDS OF TOMATOES GROWN IN THE ANDES WERE CARRIED NORTHWARD BY BIRDS AND PEOPLE TO

MEXICO

When the tomato came to Mexico, things got bigger and juicier!

Tomatoes grew well in the warm, sunny climate of Mexico. The Aztec *cultivated* (grew) a number of varieties of tomatoes there. The Aztec were a Native American people who ruled a mighty empire in Mexico during the 1400's and early 1500's.

The tomato went from a tiny berry to the large, juicy, round fruit we know today.

Tomatoes are still a major crop in Mexico to this day.

TOMATL

The Aztec called the tomato *tomatl,* meaning *swelling fruit.* This is where we got our English name for the plant.

TOMATILLO

The **tomatillo** (or Mexican husk tomato) is a relative of the tomato. It was first grown in Mexico. Its name means *little tomato* in Spanish. But tomatillos aren't tiny tomatoes! The tomatillo is a different plant. It is a small round fruit that is pale green, yellow, or purple. It has a papery husk and a tart flavor. Many are grown in Mexico and Guatemala today. The tomatillo is used a lot in Mexican **salsas.**

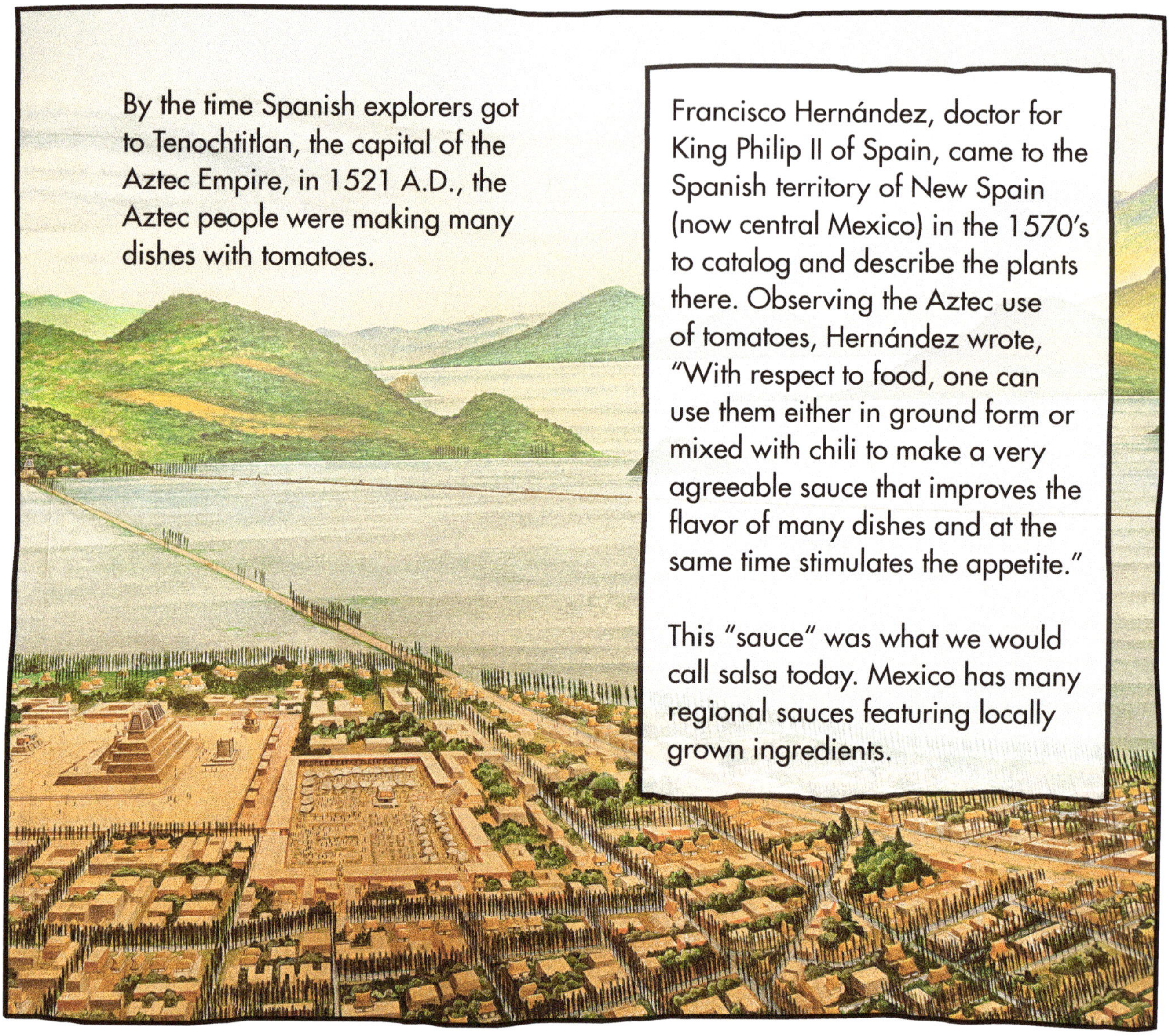

By the time Spanish explorers got to Tenochtitlan, the capital of the Aztec Empire, in 1521 A.D., the Aztec people were making many dishes with tomatoes.

Francisco Hernández, doctor for King Philip II of Spain, came to the Spanish territory of New Spain (now central Mexico) in the 1570's to catalog and describe the plants there. Observing the Aztec use of tomatoes, Hernández wrote, "With respect to food, one can use them either in ground form or mixed with chili to make a very agreeable sauce that improves the flavor of many dishes and at the same time stimulates the appetite."

This "sauce" was what we would call salsa today. Mexico has many regional sauces featuring locally grown ingredients.

SALSA

is the Spanish word for *sauce*. Before the Spanish arrived, the Aztec used the word *mōlli* to mean *sauce*. Salsas evolved as Spanish colonization and trade brought such new foods as cilantro, cumin, garlic, and limes to Mexico.

TRY THIS!

Pico de gallo is a Mexican sauce. It is similar to salsa, but salsa has more liquid in it. Pico de gallo contains very little liquid and is always made with fresh, uncooked tomatoes, onion, cilantro, and jalapeño. It can be served with other foods as a **condiment** or enjoyed as an **appetizer** with **tortilla** chips.

PICO DE GALLO

Serves 2-3

INGREDIENTS

- 1 large tomato (or 2 small), cored, seeded, and diced
- 2 tbsp. green pepper, cored, seeded, and chopped
- 1 tsp. jalapeño (optional), seeded and minced
- ¼-½ small onion, diced
- 1 clove garlic
- 1 tbsp. cilantro, chopped
- ¼ lime
- salt, to taste
- tortilla chips

STEPS

1. Place the diced tomato in a medium-sized bowl.
2. Cut the garlic clove in half, and crush it with a garlic press into the bowl of tomato.
3. Add the chopped green pepper to the bowl.
4. Add the minced jalapeño. Reduce the amount or add more if desired, to taste. *(Wear plastic gloves and be careful while handling the jalapeño—it can burn the skin. Keep away from the eyes.)*
5. Stir in the chopped cilantro.
6. Squeeze the juice from the lime quarter over the sauce. Add a pinch of salt and stir again.
7. Taste the sauce and add more salt, lime juice, garlic, or jalapeño, if desired. Eat the sauce right away or refrigerate for up to 1 day. Serve with tortilla chips.

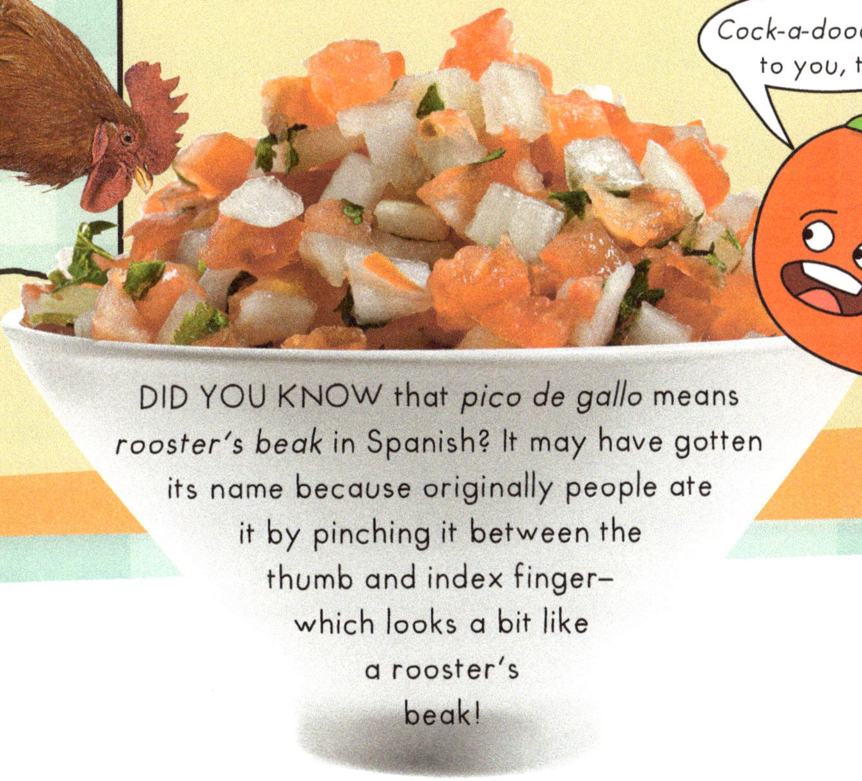

DID YOU KNOW that *pico de gallo* means *rooster's beak* in Spanish? It may have gotten its name because originally people ate it by pinching it between the thumb and index finger–which looks a bit like a rooster's beak!

IN THE MID-1500'S, THE SPANISH BROUGHT TOMATO SEEDS FROM MEXICO TO

SPAIN

Spanish explorer Hernán Cortés is thought to have brought tomatoes to Spain following his conquest of Mexico in 1521. But it took another 200 years for tomatoes to become an important part of Spanish **cuisine.** Like other Europeans, the Spanish suspected the plant was poisonous. Today, the tomato is one of the country's most important crops. A classic Spanish dish is **gazpacho,** a spicy, cold soup that includes strained tomatoes, cucumbers, olive oil, and spices.

Pan con tomate is a type of **tapa** that combines tomatoes and toasted bread. Tapas are a popular type of small dish or appetizer that is shared. Although this treat originated in Catalonia, a mountainous region in northeastern Spain, *pan con tomate* is now served all over Spain.

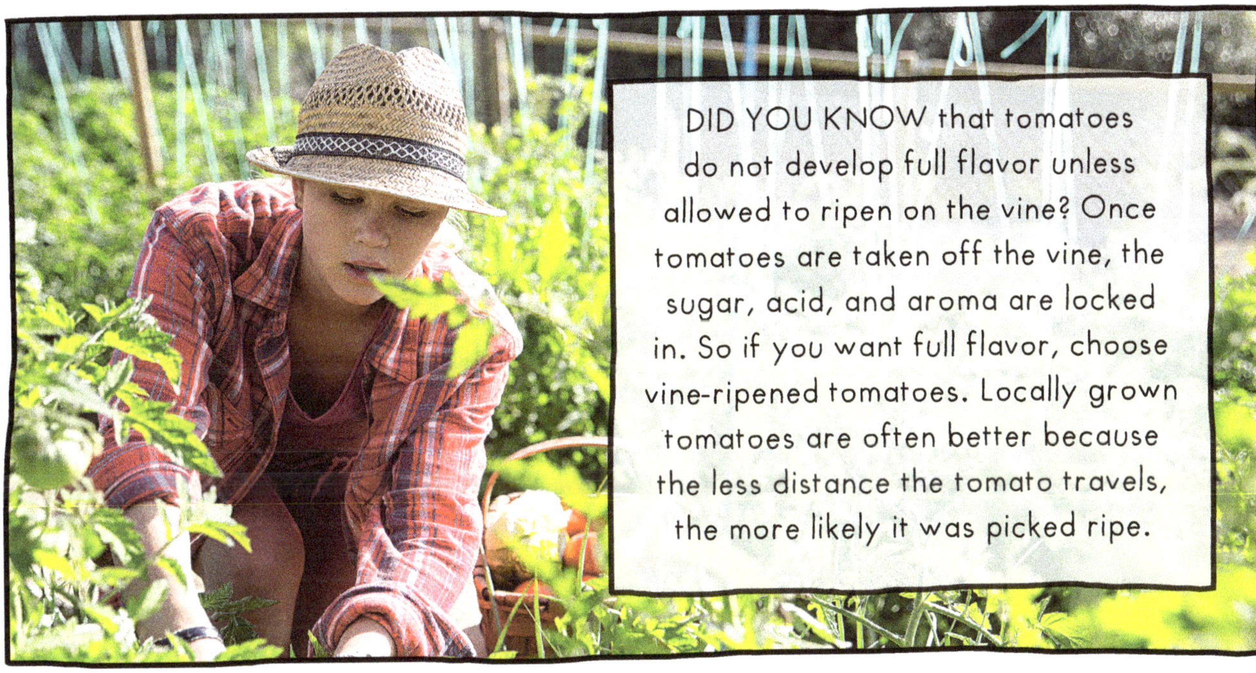

DID YOU KNOW that tomatoes do not develop full flavor unless allowed to ripen on the vine? Once tomatoes are taken off the vine, the sugar, acid, and aroma are locked in. So if you want full flavor, choose vine-ripened tomatoes. Locally grown tomatoes are often better because the less distance the tomato travels, the more likely it was picked ripe.

TRY THIS!

PAN CON TOMATE

(SPANISH TOMATO TOAST) Serves 2

INGREDIENTS

2 slices thick, crusty bread
1 clove garlic
1 vine-ripened tomato
extra-virgin olive oil
salt, to taste

STEPS

1. Toast the bread.
2. Peel the garlic clove and cut it in half. Rub the cut side of the garlic over the toasted bread. Do this while the bread is still warm. Use the other garlic half for the second slice of bread.
3. Cut the tomato in half and rub the cut side over the toasted bread, pressing firmly to push the tomato pulp into the bread, until the toast is covered with tomato (but not soggy). Discard the skins and remaining pulp.
4. Lightly drizzle the bread with olive oil and sprinkle with salt.
5. Eat right away for total toasty tomato tastiness!

FROM SPAIN, TOMATOES SPREAD TO PORTUGAL AND OTHER PARTS OF EUROPE.

FOOD FIGHT!

On the last Wednesday of August each year, thousands of people make their way from all corners of the world to the town of Buñol near Valencia, Spain, to take part in La Tomatina, the world's biggest food fight! People participate in this tomato-throwing festival for pure, messy fun! After the hour-long fight, the food fighters and the town square are covered in a slimy, red mess of crushed tomato.

SPLAT!

More than 110 tons (100 metric tons) of over-ripe tomatoes are thrown in the streets during La Tomatina!

TOMATOES SPREAD TO WHAT IS NOW NAPLES, ITALY

Spain controlled much of southern Italy in the 1500's and 1600's. The influence of Spain helped tomatoes slowly make their way into Italian cooking. Also, at the time, spices were expensive and hard to find in Italy. Tomatoes became popular in part because of their ability to flavor food.

In the 1800's, tomatoes became a regular and important part of Italian cuisine, with such classic dishes as *pasta al pomodoro.* The 1800's also saw the rise of *nationalism* (patriotic feeling) in Italy and other parts of Europe. The tomato became a symbol of Italy's cuisine. The red tomato, along with white and green foods, were prepared in dishes to represent the colors of the Italian flag.

POMODORO

The Italian name for tomato is *pomodoro.* This may have come from *pomo di moro,* which means *fruit of the Moors.* Moors are a Muslim people from northern Africa. They were thought to have introduced new foods to the Old World. Over time, *pomo di moro* may have been mistranslated as *pomo d'oro,* which means *golden apple.* (Some people believe the first tomatoes that came to Europe were yellow.)

DID YOU KNOW that one of the most famous patriotic Italian dishes is **Pizza** Margherita? The dough is layered with red tomato sauce, followed by white mozzarella cheese, then fresh green basil. The dough is stretched out and baked in a wood-fired oven. Pizza Margherita was said to have been invented in Naples to honor the Queen of Italy, Margherita of Savoy (1851-1926).

THE SAUCE IS THE SECRET!

While the tomato was used to add flavor to food in Mexico and Spain, in Italy it became the meal—in the form of tomato sauce served with **pasta.**

Tomato sauce first showed up in a *Neapolitan* (from Naples) cookbook around 1690. Its first pairing with pasta was documented in a Roman cookbook about 100 years later.

One of the simplest Italian sauces is **marinara.** It serves as the base for many other sauces. The name *marinara* comes from *marinaro,* the Italian word for *sailor.* Because this sauce could be made quickly and its ingredients could keep aboard a ship without spoiling, it is believed to have been part of Italian sailors' diets.

ONE OF A KIND

There are many different recipes for tomato sauce, and every Italian family has its favorite. No two tomato sauces are identical. This is reflected in the Sicilian expression: "He is always different, like a sauce."

DID YOU KNOW that Italy has a museum dedicated to the tomato? The Museum of Tomato is in Corti di Giarola in the province of Parma, a region historically dedicated to the production and processing of tomatoes. The museum features lots of exhibits, including a sculpture of a giant tomato!

TRY THIS!

SIMPLE MARINARA SAUCE

Serves 4

INGREDIENTS

1 28-oz. can San Marzano whole tomatoes
1 cup water
¼ cup olive oil
7 cloves garlic, thinly sliced
pinch of dried chili flakes
salt and pepper, to taste
1 large fresh basil sprig
1 1-lb. box spaghetti
Parmesan cheese, grated

STEPS

1. Pour tomatoes into a large bowl and crush them into small pieces with your hand. Place the cup of water in the empty tomato can and swish the liquid around. Add to tomatoes along with the chili flakes, salt, and pepper. (Don't over-season. You can always add more later!)
2. In a large skillet, sauté garlic in olive oil until it sizzles, about 1-2 minutes. Do not allow it to brown or the garlic will become bitter.
3. Add the bowl of tomatoes and all the liquid to the skillet. Submerge the basil sprig in the liquid.
4. Simmer until thickened, about 15-20 minutes. Remove the basil sprig.
5. Cook the spaghetti according to the instructions on the box. When done, drain, but do not rinse. Place the spaghetti in the skillet and twirl around so that all the pasta is covered with sauce.
6. Sprinkle with Parmesan cheese.

CHOOSING THE RIGHT TOMATO FOR THE JOB

Some types of tomatoes work best with certain types of dishes. Here is a handy guide to help you select the correct tomato for your recipe.

CHERRY AND GRAPE

These small gems are perfect for a bite-sized snack or an addition to a salad. But thanks to their thicker skin, they can be roasted or added to a cooked pot of pasta.

BEEFSTEAK

The large, juicy **beefsteak** is called the "king of the tomato." It is ideal for salsa or sauces. Its tender skin and mild flavor pair well with sandwiches.

PLUM

These tomatoes got their name because their oblong shape looks like that of a plum. They have fewer seeds and less water than other tomatoes. The meaty texture of plum tomatoes is ideal for making thick sauces. They are full of flavor with a bit of a tang.

SALAD

The medium-sized San Marzano tomatoes are considered the "all-purpose" tomato because they have the perfect balance of sweet and tart. They can be used for sandwiches and salads or for cooking. They are juicier than cherry or beefsteak tomatoes.

DID YOU KNOW that the San Marzano tomato is the preferred tomato used to make many traditional Italian dishes? San Marzano tomatoes come from the small town of San Marzano sul Sarno, near Naples. The San Marzano tomato is a type of plum tomato.

FROM NAPLES, TOMATOES CAME TO

FRANCE

The tomato was slow to catch on in France. It was first mentioned in a French recipe in 1797—about 200 years after it arrived in the country! Today, tomatoes are one of France's major crops.

The French prefer fresh vegetables and fruits—and the tomato is no exception! Fresh tomato is the star of one of France's most notable dishes, called **ratatouille.** This is a type of vegetable stew that originated in Nice, in Provence, France, over 100 years ago. It combines tomatoes with eggplant, zucchini, onions, and herbs. Its name comes from French words meaning *to stir up!*

The tomato shown above is one of France's most famous tomatoes. It is called the Marmande. It is named for the city in southwestern France where it was first grown in the 1890's. The Marmande weighs from 6 to 10 ounces (170 to 285 grams). Every July, the town dresses in red to honor the tomato during a two-day festival!

LOVE APPLES

A French nickname for tomatoes is *pomme d'amour,* which in French means *love apple.* This may be because of a superstition that eating them made people fall in love!

TRY THIS!

The French enjoy this classic fresh tomato tart in the summer. Cook the tomatoes until they "pop," then bake the tart upside-down! It makes a delicious appetizer or light dinner.

TOPSY-TURVY TOMATO TART

Serves 4-6

INGREDIENTS

1 tbsp. olive oil
2 pints cherry tomatoes (about 4 cups), preferably a mix of colors
salt
freshly ground black pepper
2 tbsp. balsamic vinegar
1 tsp. honey
2 tsp. chopped fresh thyme leaves
1 sheet frozen puff pastry (made with butter), thawed but still cold, corners cut off to make a 9- to 10-inch circle
goat cheese (optional)

STEPS

1. Place the oven rack in the middle of the oven. Preheat oven to 400 °F (204 °C).
2. Heat the oil in a 9- or 10-inch highly seasoned cast iron skillet over medium heat until the oil shimmers. Add the tomatoes and season with salt and pepper to taste. Cook, stirring occasionally. As the tomatoes pop, press them down gently with a spatula to release their juice. All of the tomatoes should have popped after 8 to 10 minutes. Drain the tomatoes in a colander. Let cool.
3. Add the vinegar and honey to the skillet. Bring the mixture to a simmer and cook until thick and syrupy, about 1 minute.
4. Remove the skillet from the heat. Blot tomatoes lightly with a paper towel to prevent a soggy pastry. Gently return the tomatoes to the skillet and arrange them in one layer. Sprinkle the chopped thyme over the tomatoes along with more salt and black pepper to taste.
5. Place the puff pastry circle over the tomatoes, folding under any edges. Prick the pastry with a fork.
6. Bake until the puff pastry is golden-brown, 25 to 30 minutes. Remove from the oven, let stand for 5 minutes, then run a knife around the pastry to loosen it from the skillet. When ready to serve, have an adult place a serving plate slightly bigger than the skillet over the top of it. Using oven mitts, carefully and quickly flip the tart onto the plate. Sprinkle with goat cheese if desired, and cut into wedges. Serve warm or at room temperature.

BACK ACROSS THE ATLANTIC TO THE

UNITED STATES

Even though native people in North America had been eating tomatoes for a long time, they were not popular in the United States until much later. Tomatoes may have been introduced to the area from the Caribbean. However they got there, tomatoes were being cultivated in the Carolinas by the mid-1700's. But most people only grew tomatoes in gardens as a decorative plant.

Some colonists from Europe grew and ate tomatoes, especially in some of their more *urban* (city) settlements along the Atlantic coast and the Mississippi River. So, while some people in Louisiana were enjoying tomatoes as part of a meal, others across the country in New England were growing them simply to admire in their garden!

People in most parts of the United States pronounce tomato as *tuh MAY toh*. But people in New England may pronounce it the British way: *tuh MAH toh.*

Thomas Jefferson was one of the first Virginians to grow and eat tomatoes. He grew them as early as 1781. Some scholars believe he brought them home from France. While Jefferson was president (1801-1809), tomatoes were served at presidential dinners. Jefferson later grew tomatoes at Monticello, his home near Charlottesville, Virginia. He mailed seeds from his tomatoes to leading farmers across the United States. Jefferson promoted the tomato in the United States for the rest of his life. Seeds from the tomato plants that Jefferson grew are still planted at Monticello today!

THE TOMATO DAREDEVIL

In 1820, Americans still widely believed that tomatoes were poisonous. But legend has it that Robert Gibbon Johnson, a prominent citizen of Salem, New Jersey, set out to prove otherwise. He announced that he would publicly eat a raw tomato that he had grown. Hundreds of people were said to have come to witness this shocking event. Johnson bit into a tomato, causing some onlookers to faint! But he survived. By 1830, most Americans were eating tomatoes.

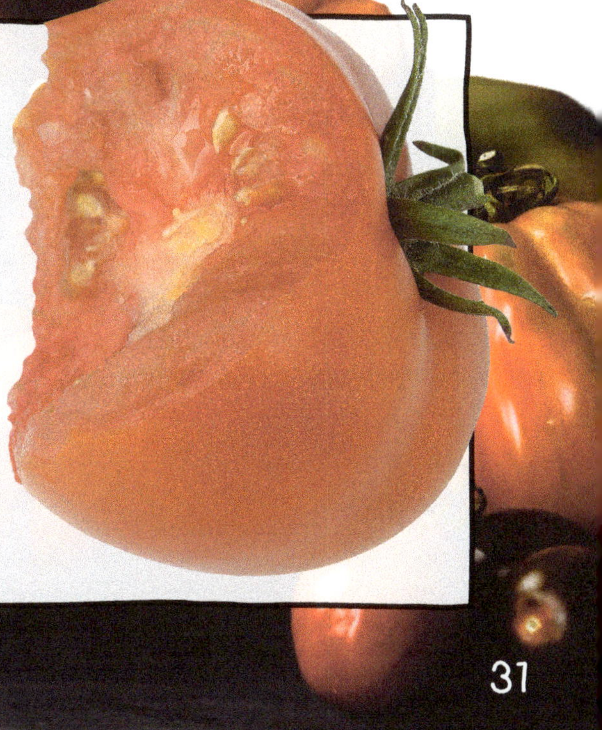

PERFECTING THE TOMATO

In the 1860's, a number of people began to breed tomatoes in the United States to try to improve them and increase production. They used seeds from selected fruits to try to grow more and better plants. But this was unsuccessful.

In 1870, Alexander W. Livingston of Reynoldsburg, Ohio, began to use seeds from entire selected plants—rather than just seeds from selected fruits—to grow larger, sweeter tomatoes. Livingston became the first person to develop the tomato into a commercially stable crop.

The paragon tomato was Livingston's first successful hybrid tomato. *Paragon* means a model of excellence. He called it "the first perfectly and uniformly smooth tomato ever introduced to the American public."

Livingston developed more than 30 other varieties of tomatoes. He helped to make tomatoes more popular with American cooks.

DID YOU KNOW that the seeds of the tomato have no flavor? The flavor comes from the gel that surrounds the seed and the meat. The skin of the tomato has a bitter taste, but it is packed with nutrients!

THE STATELY TOMATO

The tomato is the state fruit of Ohio and Tennessee. It is the state vegetable of New Jersey and Louisiana (the creole tomato). Arkansas took both sides: it declared the South Arkansas Vine Ripe Pink Tomato to be both the state fruit and vegetable!

DID YOU KNOW that tomatoes are the second most popular "vegetable" in the United States? The potato is the first. Americans eat over 20 pounds (9 kilograms) of fresh tomatoes a year.

CATCHING UP WITH

KETCHUP!

French fries with ketchup are an American favorite! But did you know that the origins of this magical sauce go back centuries to another part of the world?

The name for the sauce originated in Asia during the 1600's, from a word pronounced like *kaychup.* It may have come from the Chinese word meaning *brine of pickled fish,* or the Malay (Indonesian language of Southeast Asian peoples) word meaning *smack the lips!* It is also spelled *catsup* or *catchup.* Originally, recipes for the sauce used egg whites, mushrooms, oysters, mussels, or walnuts, among other ingredients.

But it wasn't until the addition of tomatoes that the sauce really caught on! Today's ketchup is made from tomatoes, vinegar, sugar, salt, and various spices.

DID YOU KNOW that Americans buy over 300,000 tons (270,000 metric tons) of ketchup a year? That's about 3 bottles per person! No wonder the United States has a National Ketchup Day! It is celebrated June 5.

HIGH STANDARD

The United States Food and Drug Administration has established a "Standard of Identity" for ketchup. This standard specifies what ingredients may be included in ketchup. It also specifies the standard grade of thickness for ketchup.

In 1876, Henry John Heinz, the founder of the H. J. Heinz Company, in Pittsburgh, Pennsylvania, mastered the production of a tomato sauce which was later called ketchup. The company has been famous for selling ketchup ever since.

Today, "America's national condiment" is popular around the world!

Dig in—and don't forget to use a napkin!

WORTH THE WAIT!

Heinz tomato ketchup has a speed limit! If it pours any faster than 0.028 mph, it is considered too runny and is rejected!

HOW TOMATOES MADE THEIR WAY TO

CHINA

Tomatoes came to China in the late 1500's or early 1600's. The Spanish introduced the tomato to the Philippines. From there it spread throughout Southeast Asia and other parts of Asia, including China.

At first, the Chinese did not know what to make of the tomato. They called it *xī hóng shì,* which means *western red persimmon,* or *fān qié,* which means *foreign eggplant.*

As time went on, the Chinese slowly incorporated the tomato into their diet. One popular dish is stir-fried tomatoes with scrambled eggs. The tomato, however, is not as popular in China as it is in other countries.

GROWN TO GO

China grows more tomatoes than any other country. But most of these tomatoes are not eaten—they are exported.

DID YOU KNOW that there are some areas in China where sugar is used to season tomatoes? Try making a sweet tomato salad by cutting up 4 tomatoes into bite-sized pieces and stirring in 5 tablespoons of sugar. Refrigerate for a few hours and enjoy!

A winter treat in northern China is called *tanghulu*. In ancient times, it was made with haw berries (thorn apples). But today, it can be made with any other "fruit," including tomatoes! Cherry tomatoes are stacked on a stick and then dipped into a sugary syrup which is left to harden. Biting into the crunchy exterior of the tanghulu is like biting into a candied apple!

TONS OF TOMATOES!

Today, China produces about a third of the world's supply of tomatoes—more than any other country. In a year, here's how many tomatoes are grown in the top five countries.

1 CHINA
54,311,000 tons
(49,270,000 metric tons)

2 INDIA
19,623,000 tons
(17,802,000 metric tons)

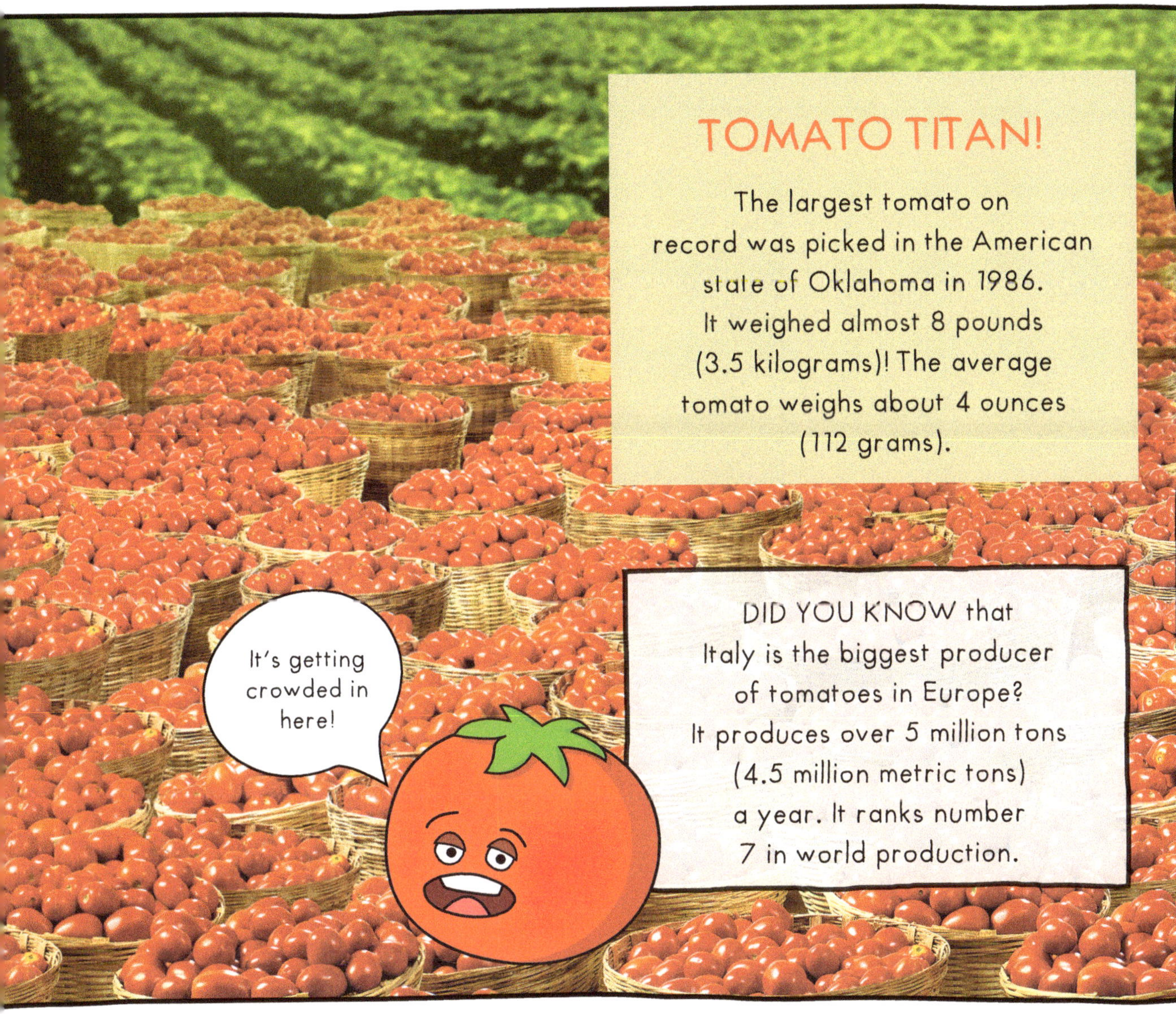

TOMATO TITAN!

The largest tomato on record was picked in the American state of Oklahoma in 1986. It weighed almost 8 pounds (3.5 kilograms)! The average tomato weighs about 4 ounces (112 grams).

DID YOU KNOW that Italy is the biggest producer of tomatoes in Europe? It produces over 5 million tons (4.5 million metric tons) a year. It ranks number 7 in world production.

3 UNITED STATES
14,076,000 tons
(12,769,000 metric tons)

4 TURKEY
12,557,000 tons
(11,391,000 metric tons)

5 EGYPT
9,283,000 tons
(8,421,000 metric tons)

IN THE 1500'S, PORTUGUESE EXPLORERS MAY HAVE INTRODUCED TOMATOES TO

INDIA

Tomatoes grow well in India's sunny, hot climate. Today, India is the second largest grower of tomatoes.

At first, tomatoes were grown in India mostly for European consumers. But Indians soon found that the tartness and sweetness of tomatoes added extra flavor to traditional Indian dishes. Some Indian groups began to use it in their **curries** (peppery sauces or stews).

DID YOU KNOW that fragrance—rather than color—is a better indicator of a tasty tomato? So when choosing a tomato, smell the stem end. If it smells good, it will taste good!

Tomatoes also appear in Indian cooking as part of the **masala** (spice blend). But they also play a starring role in other dishes, including tomato rice, tomato **chutney** (spicy sauce), tomato fry, and a famous South Indian tomato soup called *rasam*.

THE LAST PLACE TO PUT TOMATOES ON THE TABLE WAS THE

MIDDLE EAST

People in the Middle East did not eat tomatoes until well into the 1800's. The Middle East is a region that spreads across southwestern Asia and northeastern Africa.

Tomatoes grow well in the Middle East because the climate is perfectly suited to the plant's needs. The Middle Eastern country of Turkey is the fourth largest grower of tomatoes. Tomatoes are also the country's biggest export product.

Today, the tomato is an important and common part of Middle Eastern cuisine. It is served fresh in salads, such as Arab salad, Israeli salad, Shirazi salad, and Turkish salad. It is also popular in sauces and grilled with **shish kebab** (pieces of lamb, tomatoes, peppers, and onions cooked together on a skewer).

TASTES LIKE CANDY

The *tomaccio* is a type of cherry tomato introduced by plant developers in Israel. It is the result of a breeding program using wild Peruvian tomatoes. The tomaccio is a sweet snack tomato that tastes like candy when it is dried!

GROW YOUR OWN

TOMATOES!

The tastiest tomatoes are those that are picked right off the vine. Growing your own tomatoes is easy to do. All you need is a large pot, some good soil, and a warm, sunny location.

Choose a tomato plant that can grow in a container. A patio or bush variety is best because these will not grow as tall as other varieties.

Choose a deep container that is about 20 inches (51 centimeters) in diameter, with drainage holes on the bottom.

Partially fill the container with high-quality potting soil. Place the tomato in the center and continue filling the container with dirt. Adjust the plant as necessary so that the roots are covered with dirt. Insert three stakes around the plant. As your plant grows, tie the stems to the stakes.

Keep the plant watered so that the soil stays moist, but not soggy. Water the plant at the dirt line, making sure that the leaves and fruit do not get wet.

Place your plant in a sunny location where the plant can get 6 to 8 hours of sunlight. Apply a fertilizer according to package instructions. Talk with your local garden center about which fertilizer is best for your tomatoes.

FULL OF VITAMINS

Tomatoes are a good source of vitamins A and C.

The world's largest tomato tree was grown in an experimental greenhouse at Epcot, Walt Disney World Resort, near Orlando, Florida, in 2016. It produced more than 32,000 tomatoes in the first 16 months after it was planted, and holds the record for producing the most tomatoes in a single year, according to the *Guinness Book of World Records*.

OUT OF THIS WORLD!

With over 10,000 varieties of tomatoes, you never know where one might turn up!

In 1984, NASA sent more than 12.5 million tomato seeds into space aboard the space shuttle Challenger. Astronauts launched the seeds in canisters into orbit from the shuttle. They were retrieved six years later by the space shuttle Columbia. The seeds were then distributed to schoolchildren around the world. They planted the seeds and found that the space tomatoes were just as healthy as tomatoes that never left Earth! In some cases, the space tomatoes were even tastier, juicier, and sweeter!

DID YOU KNOW that one day colonists may dine on fresh tomatoes on Mars? Researchers are growing tomatoes in the extreme weather of Antarctica to test the ability to grow food in Mars-like conditions.

CELEBRATE THE TOMATO!

October is National Tomato Month in the United States. National Fresh Tomato Day is observed on April 6.

GLOSSARY

appetizer *(AP uh TY zuhr)* The first part of a meal.

beefsteak *(BEEF STAYK)* **tomato** One of the largest varieties of cultivated tomatoes.

chutney *(CHUHT nee)* A spicy sauce or relish made of fruits, herbs, pepper, and other seasoning.

condiment *(KON duh muhnt)* Something used to give flavor and relish to food.

cuisine *(kwih ZEEN)* A style of cooking or preparing food.

curry *(KUR ee)* A peppery sauce made from a mixture of spices, seeds, and turmeric. Curry is a popular seasoning in India.

gazpacho *(gahth PAH choh* or *gahs PAH choh)* A cold soup made of strained tomatoes, cucumbers, garlic, olive oil, onions, and spices.

heirloom *(AIR LOOM)* An older variety of a plant group.

hybrid *(HY brihd)* The offspring of two different things.

ketchup *(KEHCH uhp)* (also spelled **catsup** or **catchup**) A food-seasoning sauce made from tomatoes, vinegar, sugar, salt, and various spices.

marinara *(MAR uh NAR uh)* A sauce flavored with tomatoes and garlic, used in Italian cuisine.

masala *(mah SAH lah)* A blend of spices used in Indian cooking.

pasta *(PAHS tah)* A food made from wheat and water, such as spaghetti or macaroni.

pico de gallo *(PEEK oh day GYE oh)* A sauce or condiment made of fresh, uncooked tomatoes, onion, cilantro, and jalapeño.

pizza *(PEET suh)* A flat bread dough usually topped with cheese, tomato sauce, and herbs.

ratatouille *(RAD uh TOO ee)* A type of vegetable stew or casserole.

salsa *(SAHL sah)* A hot sauce served especially with Mexican or Southwestern food.

shish kebab *(SHIHSH kuh BOB)* Pieces of lamb, tomatoes, peppers, and onions cooked together on a skewer.

tapa *(TAH puh)* A small dish or appetizer that is shared.

tomatillo *(toh muh TEE oh)* A small round fruit, of pale green, yellow, or purple color with a papery husk.

tortilla *(tawr TEE yuh)* A thin, round flatbread made from corn meal or flour.

variety *(vuh RY uh tee)* A division of a kind of living thing.

HELPFUL HINTS

When working in the kitchen with food, keep these helpful hints in mind to make sure your work goes smoothly and safely. Then enjoy the tasty treats you make!

- **Wash your hands** before you begin food preparation and after you've touched raw eggs or meat.
- Thoroughly **wash fruits and vegetables.**
- **Use oven mitts** when handling hot pots, pans, or trays.
- **Have an adult help** when working with knives and hot stoves or ovens.

INDEX

World Book, Inc.
180 North LaSalle Street
Suite 900
Chicago, Illinois 60601
USA

For information about other "Taste the World!" titles, as well as other World Book print and digital publications, please go to www.worldbook.com.

For information about other World Book publications, call 1-800-WORLDBK (967-5325).

For information about sales to schools and libraries, call 1-800-975-3250 (United States) or 1-800-837-5365 (Canada).

Library of Congress Cataloging-in-Publication Data

Title: Tomato.
Description: Chicago, Illinois: World Book Inc., [2020] | Series: Taste the world! | Includes index. | Contents: I am tomato! -- What is a tomato? -- A closer look at the tomato plant -- Types of tomatoes -- South America -- Mexico -- Spain -- Food fight! -- Italy -- The sauce is the secret! -- Choosing the right tomato for the job -- France -- United States -- Perfecting the tomato -- Catching up with ketchup! -- China -- Tons of tomatoes! -- India -- Middle East -- Grow your own tomatoes! -- Out of this world!
Identifiers: LCCN 2019037375 | ISBN 9780716628668 (hardcover) | ISBN 9780716628583 (set)
Subjects: LCSH: Tomatoes--History--Juvenile literature. | Cooking (Tomatoes)--Juvenile literature.
Classification: LCC SB349 .T615 2020 | DDC 635/.642--dc23
LC record available at https://lccn.loc.gov/2019037375

Taste the World!
ISBN: 978-0-7166-2858-3 (set, hc.)

Tomato
ISBN: 978-0-7166-2866-8 (hc.)

Also available as:
ISBN: 978-0-7166-2874-3 (e-book)

2nd printing July 2020

STAFF

Editorial

Writer: Shawn Brennan

Manager, New Product Development
Nick Kilzer

Proofreader: Nathalie Strassheim

Manager, Contracts and Compliance (Rights and Permissions): Loranne K. Shields

Manager, Indexing Services
David Pofelski

Digital

Director, Digital Product Development
Erika Meller

Digital Product Manager
Jonathan Wills

Graphics and Design

Coordinator, Design Development and Production
Brenda Tropinski

Senior Visual Communications Designer
Melanie Bender

Media Editor: Rosalia Bledsoe

Senior Web Designer/Digital Media Developer
Matt Carrington

Manufacturing/Production

Manufacturing Manager: Anne Fritzinger

Production Specialist: Curley Hunter

ACKNOWLEDGMENTS

Cover © Focus and Blur/Shutterstock; © Stacey Ventura, StockFood/age fotostock
Character artwork by Matthew Carrington
2-3 © Shutterstock; Public Domain; © Stacey Ventura, StockFood/age fotostock
4-11 © Shutterstock
12-13 © Olga Kot Photo/Shutterstock; © Arco Images GmbH/Alamy Images; © Freedom Naruk/Shutterstock
14-15 © Shutterstock
16-17 © M.Sobreira, Alamy Images; Public Domain; © S Oleg/Shutterstock; © Debbi Smirnoff, iStockphoto
18-19 © Vitaly Korovin, Shutterstock; © Russ Rohde, Getty Images; © Nito/Shutterstock
20-21 © Iakov Filimonov, Shutterstock
22-23 © DeAgostini/Getty Images; © Sad444/Dreamstime; © Shutterstock
24-25 © Visiva Studio/Shutterstock; © Stacey Ventura, StockFood/age footstock; © Toni Spagone, Alamy Images
26-27 © Mara Ze, Shutterstock; © Volosina/Shutterstock; © Astrida/iStockphoto; © Luigi Giordano, Shutterstock; © Tatuasha/Shutterstock
28-29 © Ronald Sumners, Shutterstock; © FoodCollection/age fotostock
30-31 © Casanisa/Shutterstock; *Thomas Jefferson* (1800), oil on canvas by Rembrandt Peale; White House Collection; © Elena Kitch, Shutterstock
32-33 Smithsonian Institution; © Tim Ur, Shutterstock
34-35 © Shutterstock
36-37 © Luis Portugal/iStockphoto; © Handmade Pictures/Shutterstock; © A Photo Story/Shutterstock
38-39 © Shutterstock
40-41 © Rob Elliott, Getty Images; © Monebook/Shutterstock; © Corlaffra/Shutterstock; © Chameleons Eye/Shutterstock
42-43 © Lux Pics/Shutterstock; © Yuri Samsonov, Shutterstock; © Pat Canova, Alamy Images
44-45 NASA/JSC; NASA/Pat Rawlings; © Sudowoodo/Shutterstock

www.ingramcontent.com/pod-product-compliance
Ingram Content Group UK Ltd.
Pitfield, Milton Keynes, MK11 3LW, UK
UKHW061957290726
14090UKWH00021B/1255

9 780716 647683